Becom... in Your Own Skin

Tuwana Nicole

Printed in the United States of America

The Library of Congress Cataloging-in-Publication
Data:

Application for cataloging has been submitted at
the time of print.

ISBN-13: 978-1974683000

ISBN-10: 1974683001

Unless otherwise stated, Scripture is taken from
The NIV/Message Parallel Study Bible (NIV) (MSG)

All quotes by others have been given credit within
actual quotes.

Definitions taken from Wikipedia

Book cover designed by Pasindu Lakshan

Book Interior Design, Format, and Publishing by
Tuwana Nicole

Dedication

This book is dedicated to memory of my mother, Elnora. Thank you for introducing me to God. I miss you every day.

My future husband. Thank you for praying for, pursuing, supporting, believing, and being patient with me as I become the best version of myself.

To my children, Kashun and Kennedy: Your very existence has pushed me to never give up no matter how hard life can be sometimes.

To everyone who told me that I would never amount to anything, called me crazy, counted me out, put me down, broke my heart, used me; I just want to thank you because you helped me learn how to become comfortable in my own skin.

A special thank you to the following people who have made it possible for others struggling with their identity and self-worth to receive a FREE copy of this book: my best friend Maranda and my business partner and friend Lynnette.

Last, but certainly not least:

To my heavenly Father who has made all things possible. There aren't enough words to express my gratitude for you being my protector, provider, way-maker, healer, comforter, my EVERYTHING! I love you God!

Contents

Contents

Part 2

The Body

Contents

Part 3

The Soul

Contents

Introduction

We live in a society that tells you that you have to look a certain way, be a particular size, have a husband/wife, and 2.5 children to be acceptable. Sadly, even the church has accepted many of society's standards. One must ask the question, who came up with these standards? Although some situations may position you better in our society, they should never become standards to how you view yourself. God made each of us uniquely and that should be the standard that you accept for yourself.

The goal of this book is to help you learn how to successfully become comfortable in your own skin. Having a good understanding of who you are will help you to accept your uniqueness, embrace, and celebrate it in every aspect of your life with authenticity.

I haven't always been comfortable in my own skin. For many years I was caught up in a religious system that focused more on changed behavior than a changed heart; following rules rather than learning who

God was. It made me think that God only loved me if I acted a certain way and obeyed a certain set of rules. I struggled with low esteem, what people thought of me, and was anxious to fit in. It took me years to get to the place where I could love myself unconditionally. Once I began to accept myself, my life started improving in every aspect: my relationships, my business, and my ministry. All because I no longer had to wear a mask. I could be authentically and unapologetically me!

As I get older, I have begun to notice more and more people struggling to be themselves, going through unnecessary heartaches, angry, and just overall unhappy with their lives. After going through many years feeling the same way, I could no longer look the other way when I see others in pain.

Having struggled with wearing masks for many years myself, I wanted to make it easier for others to have a little go to guide to make their process easier than what it had been for me. There was a lot of trial and error getting to where I am now, but it has led me to a better than blessed life.

Everyday isn't perfect and I continue to be a work in progress while embracing who/where I am right now in this very moment. That is my hope for you.

Know that becoming comfortable in your own skin is not an overnight process. It is a life-long process of loving and accepting yourself just the way God made you. It doesn't matter what your skin color is, the age you are, or if you are male or female; if you haven't dealt with the issues from your past, they will continue to haunt you.

There will always be some areas you can and should improve on. I definitely encourage that, but never make changes simply to please someone else or allow anyone to make you feel like you don't have value because you don't fit into their standards. The way you look, how much money you have in the bank, the car you drive, or the clothes you wear should never be main focal points in your life.

There may be some places that reading this book will take you mentally and spiritually that you may not be ready to go to. It may bring back painful memories from your past, but I ask that you trust the process. After reading this book, you should be able to begin and/or move forward in your process to becoming comfortable in your own skin.

Prayerfully, you will gain powerful insight from my personal experiences and begin to recognize God's plan for your life. I hope you be able to relate to some of my stories and avoid some of the pitfalls that I have made over the years. If you're personally unable to relate, maybe you have a friend, family member, or client that has experienced or is experiencing some of the things that I have and by reading this book, you will be able to understand what they are going through.

Each chapter is representative to my age(s) in which I encountered each experience. This book is detailed, but for the purpose intended; it doesn't go in depth about every experience I have encountered. My autobiography entitled "From Rejected To Redeemed", will be coming out next year. It will go more in depth about my life and how I overcame.

Feel free to write in answers to some of the questions that I present at the end of each chapter or take notes to go back to for future reference. If this book has helped you, pass it on to someone else you know who may benefit from reading it.

"Like an open book, you watched me grow from conception to birth; all the stages of my life were spread out before you. The days of my life all prepared before I'd even lived one day."

Psalm 139:16 MSG

Part 1

The Mind

The mind is a set of cognitive faculties including consciousness, perception, thinking, judgement, and memory.

"The mind governed by the flesh is death, but the mind governed by the Spirit is life and peace."

Romans 8:6 NIV

Step 1

Sit in Your Truth

"You can't do anything as long as you are afraid of what might happen. Fear clouds opportunities, erases possibilities, and limits the ability to move beyond the place in which the mind is stuck. No matter how difficult we think the problem is, we must muster up the courage to face it."
Iyanla Vanzant

Before you can begin the process to becoming comfortable in your own skin, you must do a reality check and sit in your truth. Own where you are currently in your life today. Understand that sitting in your truth may be very difficult at first. Prayerfully as I share some of my personal experiences with you, you will become empowered to walk it out.

Trust yourself enough to believe that no matter what life has thrown your way, you can get through it. Recognize that this process is about YOU, not anyone else. It's going to take time. This is a necessary step to beginning the healing process. Otherwise, you will continue to recycle the same experiences. You cannot heal what you won't reveal. God cannot bless what you will not confess.

Is there any baggage from your childhood that you are carrying around with you? Allow the little boy/girl in you to speak. Listen to what he/she is saying, then acknowledge it. Acknowledge the pain. Then allow him/her to cry. Stop blaming the little boy/girl in you for not being able to process your pain earlier. Until you learn to accept your past, it will remain a driving force in your present life.

Stop simply surviving, let's learn how to thrive together! As I share my story, begin writing yours.

As you begin this process, please
remember:

*"The end of a matter is
better than its beginning,
and patience is better than
pride."*
Ecclesiastes 7:8-9 NIV

Notes

Chapters 0-2

From the Beginning

"Before I shaped you in the womb, I knew all about you. Before you saw the light of day, I had holy plans for you:
A prophet to the nations-that's what I had in mind for you."
Jeremiah 1:5 MSG

The mind is very powerful. It's amazing what your mind can remember, rationalize, perceive, and suppress at such a young age. I am still unsure of how I suppressed so much pain to get through life and fair as well as I did.

I firmly believe that in order to get to the end of a matter, you must start at the beginning. I started suppressing my pain from the time I was born. I didn't realize that everything I did for the next 32 years was a direct result of how my life had begun.

As a baby, I automatically knew who God was. The problem was understanding who He was supposed to be to me. After reading this scripture and thinking about my childhood, I used to think there was no way that God could've formed me in my mother's womb. There was no way He could have a plan for my life. I feared God, His rejection, and wrath because I couldn't understand why He created me.

Here's how my life began:

My mother was married to my siblings' Father, but was having an affair with my Father. As a result of this adulterous relationship, she became pregnant with me. So here I was conceived in sin, born in sin, and destined to live a life of sin!

It's pretty hard to believe that anything good, or in my case any good human could come from something that was so wrong. I was an illegitimate bastard from the beginning. How could God love me? How could He possibly have a plan for my life?

Around age 2, I was hospitalized because I had contracted a sexually transmitted disease. You mean to tell me that God knew me? There was no way. If God has such great plans for me, how could He allow someone to molest me? I was just a baby!! And where was my Mother and Father? If they loved me, why didn't they protect me?

At age 2, my Father moved away because of issues stemming from his adulterous relationship with my Mother. I already knew God and my Mother didn't love me, but now my Dad too? The only thing that kept me going during this time was being adored by everyone because I was so cute! Everybody loved to kiss my chubby cheeks. Being the youngest of six children really helped me get through these years.

Questions for Reflection

Do you remember being a baby?

What do you remember about it?

How does thinking back make you feel after reading about my early life?

Can you relate to my story? How?

Do you have any unresolved issues from when you were born? If so, write them here:

Did reading about my early years bring back any suppressed memories from your childhood? Explain.

Chapters 3-5

What About Me?

"How long Lord? Will you forget me forever? How long will you hide your face from me?"
Psalm 13:1

With my Father gone, now my oldest sister decides to get married. I'm only 4 years old and you decide to take away the only person that loves me!? Ok God! You said that you knew me, and had a plan for me? How does this fit into your plan? Why is everyone I love leaving me? No, why is everyone who is supposed to love me forgetting about me? Even you God, you made me, so why are you allowing my little life to be so miserable?

We had a railroad track in front of our house. One of my older sisters used to sit me on the railroad tracks and throw rocks at me for sport. On another occasion, my Mother beat me with an extension cord because someone stole her cigarette money from me while I walking to the store to get them for her. I just wanted to be loved, but it seemed like I was in everyone's way. My life didn't have value.

I was the mistake, the sin, the illegitimate bastard, the different one.

My siblings always teased me about my nose. I never developed cartilage in the bridge of my nose, so it is flat. They would tell me that I looked like an elephant had stepped on my nose. I always felt they made fun of me because I had a different Father. These experiences made me feel rejected. I began to believe that I would never be good enough.

Though I was suffering, God was still at work in my life. I thought I was losing my big sister, but her getting married was the best thing that could've happened to me. God had a plan all along. It took me many years to understand God's plan for my life, but it was at this tender age that my family starting going to church. I finally was introduced to God through His Word, the Bible.

I really liked being in a church environment. I loved my Bible School teachers. I learned songs like "Jesus Loves Me" and "This Little Light of Mine". Over the next few years, my life seemed to get better. I began to think, God does love me, but for how long….

Questions for Reflection

Did you grow up in a church environment?

Do you think it's wrong to question God? Why? Explain your logic.

Did you grow up with both parents?

If not, how did growing up with one parent affect you?

Did you feel like God has forgotten about you? Why/why not?

Do you feel like you're in the way or out of place in your family? At school? Explain.

Has anyone ever called you names? How did it make you feel?

Step 2

Think Positive

"Just like a closed heart can't receive love, a negative mind can't learn. Be open to the possibilities."
Tuwana Nicole

From the beginning I had negative thoughts. I had no control as to how my life began nor what was happening to me during my childhood. I lived in such a negative environment, I never even thought that there was an issue with my thinking. My mind wasn't even mature enough to see that God was revealing Himself to me. I just thought that this was how my life was going to be. I didn't realize how negative my self-talk was until I was in my 20's.

I was so critical of everything about me because of how my life had begun. I never felt truly loved by anyone so I didn't know how to love myself. My thoughts about myself made me doubt everything about myself and those around me. Subconsciously, I treated myself the exact same way that I had been treated by others.

I had so many hopes and dreams, but they continued to be overshadowed by my environment. I wrote many stories and songs in my young teens. But as I grew older, the harder it was for me to think positive. I stopped believing that I could one day own my own business, write several books, or help others.

I had always been an avid reader. I was always seeking knowledge. I would buy different self-help and spiritual books to help with my thinking. Even though I really didn't have a relationship with God at this point in my life; positive thinking had a huge impact on me.

The very things that we say we don't want, have a way of manifesting themselves in our lives. For every negative thought, I would try think the opposite. I would tell myself over and over, I am somebody. I am important. I am beautiful. I am talented. I am smart. I can do this.

Knowledge is power, but only if you use it. I struggled for many years to think more positively, but it helped me to begin the process of becoming comfortable in my own skin. I encourage you to do the same thing.

Here are a few ways you can begin to think more positively:
1. For every negative thought that you have about yourself, write down the complete opposite.
2. Read books that are empowering.
3. Write down positive quotes and sayings.
4. Repeat over and over again these simple affirmations: I am

somebody. I am smart. I can do this., etc.

Questions for Reflection

What is your thinking like?

Are you always thinking the worst or do you have a positive outlook?

Do you say things to yourself like: I'm stupid, I'm fat, or I'm ugly? I will never find a good man. Or things never work out for me? What do you plan to do to change this?

Remember to replace your negative thoughts with positive ones. Put positive sayings on sticky notes on your headboard, bathroom mirror, or dashboard.

Chapters 12-13

Is that You God?

"Teach me to do your will, for you are my God; may your good Spirit lead me on level ground."
Psalm 143:10 NIV

After years of praying and asking God to help me, asking why nobody loved me; at age 12 something happened. I began to have an overwhelming urge to read books on breaking the cycle of dysfunction and looking for love in all the wrong places. God was using different books to help me deal with my feelings and to understand why I was even feeling the way I was. At the time I didn't realize it, but God was speaking to me through the Holy Spirit.

God had always been there through the good, the bad, and the ugly; unfortunately I still struggled to really know Him. After feeling rejected by almost everyone that I knew, it was really hard to believe that God wouldn't reject me too! Besides I had heard on too many Sundays how I was going to die and go to hell if I didn't get baptized.

Out of fear and curiosity at age 13, I got baptized. I know it wasn't the church's intentions to scare people into getting baptized, but it definitely didn't help me get to know God better. In fact, I spent the next few years wondering why God hadn't shown up in my life. I kept wondering, where are you God? Why is my life still the same? I thought if I got baptized, you would accept me and not reject me? What happened?

Now I felt like God was rejecting me just like my Father had. I had written my Father many letters over the years. Either one of two things happened; I didn't get a response back from him or when I did get one, it was months later.

Even though my Father was absent, my paternal Grandparents were the best! They always made sure that I was included and part of the family. Even as I write this book, I have never felt more love from any other human beings like my Grandparents loved me. They did the best they could to fill the void, but I still longed for the love that only my Father could give.

Despite God revealing Himself to me; I still couldn't receive Him because I never felt truly loved, church doctrine, my non-existent relationship with my Father, my feelings that no one understood me, and the environment that I lived in. I realize now that everyone around me was doing the best they could trying to manage their own life. I wanted my life to change so badly, but I was still ill-equipped to understand how to move forward. My life continued the way it always had.

My reality doesn't have to be your reality. Let's continue to walk through some of those hard questions that you may be dealing with. In order to get your breakthrough, you must deal with our feelings. Allow yourself to feel whatever is going on with you.

Questions for Reflection

Have you ever prayed hard for something and it seemed your prayers were never answered?

Do you struggle with knowing who God is? Explain.

Have you ever felt a nudge from God? Explain.

How has your upbringing affected who you are today?

Is there anything from your childhood that you would change if you were given the opportunity? Why/Why not?

Was your Father present in your life growing up? How did that affect you?

Does your relationship with your Father affect your understanding of God? Explain.

Do you find yourself pushing people away who try to love you away? Explain.

Chapters 14-17

Still Looking For Love and Acceptance

"When I was a child, I talked like a child, I reasoned like a child. When I became a (wo)man, I put the ways of childhood behind me."
1 Corinthians 13:11 NIV

Coming into my teenage years, I still experienced lots of ridicule from my siblings and at school. They called me black Dolly Parton because my breasts developed quicker than theirs did. They teased me about having book sense, but no common sense. If the name calling wasn't bad enough, I was constantly ridiculed about my Father's side of the family having mental issues. I really didn't realize or understand how all these "little" things affected my self-esteem and self-worth until my Being Mary Jane years.

Many situations/relationships that we find ourselves in are simply a reflection of how we feel about ourselves. At age 15 I met my first love. He told me that he loved me and wanted to marry me. His words were like music to my ears. I had waited my entire life for someone to tell me and show me that they loved me.

At the time, I didn't know that the love that he had to give was purely based on physical attraction. Honestly; I should have known better because other girls had told me that he tried to get with them, but my fear of being rejected made me delusional to my reality.

After many months of saying no to this physical advances, one night I gave in. I was tired of him pressuring me and I didn't want to lose him. Up until this point, he had treated me the way I wanted to be treated. He wrote me cute love notes, bought me perfume, took me to the movies, and gave me money for snacks. Plus he had a good job, what more could a girl ask for right!?

Because of my church background, I knew it was wrong to have sex before marriage. But he told me he was going to marry me so in the back of my head I said, here is your chance for love. I was still looking for love and acceptance.

Not long after we were intimate, I missed my monthly cycle. Then I missed it the next month too. Scared and unsure what to do, I asked my closest cousin what would make me miss my cycle. She bought me a pregnancy test from her job and it was positive! Oh boy, how am I going to break this to my Mother? She is going to kill me? How could I be pregnant when I wasn't even allowed to date?

It wasn't too hard for my Mother to figure it out. I was talking to an older sister one day on the phone and that's exactly what happened. She asked, Tuwana are you pregnant? All I could do was cry. I already didn't feel loved by my Mother, now I've got to hear her mouth. Before long everyone in my family knew about my pregnancy.

To make matters worse, my Father tells me that I messed up my life and I'll never amount to anything. My Mother tells me I have to quit school to take care of the baby. My oldest sister tells me I should've learned from her and two of my other older sisters' mistakes. Each of them had a child at a young age and weren't married when their children were born.

Once the church got wind of my pregnancy; they put me in the adult Bible Study class because they didn't want me to be a bad influence on the other girls. I'm like are you kidding me? I was the last of the girls I grew up with to start having sex. Several girls I knew had already had abortions, so no one knew they were sinning. I was just the first one to get caught on my first attempt!

I was already dealing with the rejection of everyone I know, the last person I expected to reject me was my baby's Father! I'm sure you guessed it. He rejected me too. He denied our son my whole pregnancy. So here I am living with the harsh reality that I am just like everyone else in my family. I am repeating the same cycle that my Mother and sisters did. Here I am a bastard about to have a bastard! Here I am an unwed, teenage mother with very little support.

I'm right back to that newborn baby asking God, how could you possibly have a plan for my life? All I ever wanted was love and acceptance, but here I am still being rejected!

Everyone thought I should have known better, but no one had shown me how to do better. I cried out for help, but I had made my bed hard so now I had to sleep in it. The time had come for me to put on my big girl panties. I was no longer a child. I had to become a woman real fast because I had a baby boy coming in less than six months!

My son was born on April 6, 1992. I had just turned 17 the month before. Still a child myself, but now with a child of my own to raise. Thankfully; I had formed a tight bond with my son's Grandmother. She really embraced me during this difficult time in my life and for the rest of her life. She made sure her son came to the hospital and signed the birth certificate. I'll never forget her love and kindness. She was one of the sweetest people I

have ever met. She was an angel
sent to help me get through this
difficult stage in my life.

Questions for Reflection

Can you relate to my situation? Do
you see yourself in any part of my
story? Explain.

Are you looking for love and
acceptance? Explain.

Did you have to learn how to be
an adult before you could finish
being a child? Explain.

Have you ever been pressured to
have sex? Explain.

What would you have done differently if you were in my same situation?

How do you know you would've handled things differently?

Do/did you have a support system when you were growing up? Explain.

Have you noticed a pattern in your family? Is it good or bad? Explain.

Step 3
Get to know YOU!
"Go after a life of self-love."
Tuwana Nicole

I had spent so much time looking for love, acceptance, and prioritizing others that I didn't even know who I was. I had defined myself based on others' opinion of me instead of my opinion of myself. I had developed a life that was only as important as the people that I had surrounded myself with. I realized that I needed to take time to get to know Tuwana.

Take some time daily to be with yourself. Be good to yourself and treat yourself to that vacation that you've always wanted to take, but the time has never been right. You may want to journal some of your thoughts. Think about who you are, how you view yourself, where you are in life, things you have accomplished, and what type of legacy you would like to leave. Begin to make small steps toward getting to know you better because if you don't know who you are or don't enjoy your own company, how could you possibly expect someone to? If you don't love yourself, how can you expect anyone else to!?

If there are people, places and things that you need to remove from your life to become a better version of yourself; by all means do it! But, don't change so people will like you. Change because you want to. Change because you want to become a better person. Change because you want to be true to yourself. Always be yourself and the right people will love the real you.

On my journey to getting to know myself, I began to do things that I had always wanted to do. I did things that I wouldn't dare do by myself because I never felt comfortable enough in my own skin to do it. I starting taking trips to places that I only wanted to go to with a significant other. I starting taking myself out to lunch, dinner, or to the movies.

You have to be completely honest with yourself if you want to heal. Would you want to hang out with yourself? Can you go to the movies or dinner by yourself? If you struggle with being alone or doing things by yourself then you may not be comfortable in your own skin.

As you begin to spend time with God, you will realize whose you are and who you are and that you are never alone. He will guide your steps on a daily basis if you allow Him to. We will talk more about developing a relationship with God a little later.

Questions for Reflection

Do you know who you are?

Who are you? How would you describe yourself?

Do you like who you are? Why/why not?

Do you see some areas that need improvement?

What steps are you taking to get to know yourself better?

How did you answer some of the questions posed within the chapter?

Is there any baggage from your past that you are still carrying around with you? Explain.

Part 2
The Body

The physical and mortal aspect of a person as opposed to the soul or spirit.

"Therefore I urge you brothers and sisters, by mercies of God, to present your bodies {dedicating all of yourselves, set apart} as a living sacrifice, holy and pleasing to God, which is your rational (logical, intelligent) act of worship."
Romans 12:1 AMP

Chapters 17.5-22
REJECTION Sucks!

"If you live by the approval of others, you will die by their rejection."
Rick Warren

At the beginning of my senior year, I secretly started dating a longtime friend and classmate. My Mother still didn't allow me to date. He had always had a crush on me so it was an instant love connection. I had never been given the love and attention that he gave me. He was great with my son and had the family that I always wanted to be a part of. Before you knew it, we were head over heels in love. He was my EVERYTHING and the undisputed love of my life! I knew he was the man that I was going to spend the rest of my life with. I began to put him on a pedestal that was only meant for God.

As graduation and prom drew near, he broke up with me saying that he wanted to go to the prom with someone else. At the last minute, he came back and decided to take me to the prom. That night I became pregnant. He wanted to keep the baby, but I didn't because by this time, I had experienced enough REJECTION to last me a lifetime. He had already broken up with me once so a baby sure wouldn't keep him from doing it again. We went through with the abortion.

He finally asked me to marry him after 2 years of dating, but I couldn't. Plus he didn't even give me a ring! Subconsciously, I feared being rejected again. I couldn't be sure that he was going to be there for me. We dated off and on for many years; saying we would get married one day, but we never did. We both had our share of issues, but I always thought we would work everything out in the end.

The heartbreak of this relationship made me numb. I began to develop a tough skin in order to protect my feelings. I had other relationships, but I didn't really trust anyone anymore with my heart because all I got in the end was REJECTION! I was always looking for him in every guy that I dated. Even though he had lied and cheated on me on numerous occasions, he still had treated me better than any other male had. I subconsciously convinced myself that I would never find a love like this again. I was so broken and needy, He could do no wrong in my eyes. I had made him my God (idol).

From being molested as a baby to being pressured to have sex, and now not being good enough to keep the devotion of the undisputed love of my life. I began to believe that sex was the only thing that I was good for. I still wanted to be loved, but subconsciously knew I would never get it so I began to accept that this was just the way it was.

My mind couldn't rationalize my feelings of emptiness so I used my body to get what I wanted from men. God sent some amazing men my way, but I couldn't accept them because I was still carrying the burden of our broken relationship. I still didn't know who I was and didn't love myself.

I didn't realize at the time, but I desired the same type of relationship with him that I had desired from God. I thought that he was going to be my hero, my savior, my finally. But he turned out to be just like God, my Father, and my son's Father had been……nowhere to be found when I needed them!

Just like everything else that I had experienced in life, I carried these burdens of rejection for many years always believing that somehow it was my fault because

I never should've been born in the first place. In the end, this rejection was a major key to helping me understand the importance of becoming comfortable in my own skin.

Questions for Reflection

Do you sometimes wish you had never been born? Explain.

Do you see the correlation between my relationship with God and everyone else in my life? How can you relate in your own life experiences? Explain.

Have you been looking for someone to save you? Explain.

Have you ever put a
relationship/person on a pedestal?
Explain.

How did the relationship turn out?

Have you ever been rejected?
Explain about a time you were
rejected and how you handled it.

Do you feel like you have
learned/grown from being
rejected? Explain.

Step 4

Take Care of YOU!

*"Don't allow your love for others
to diminish your love of self."*
Tuwana Nicole

As women, many times we're looking out for everyone else, except ourselves. We are constantly putting others needs before our own because we are natural nurturers. Men, I'm not forgetting about you! I know you can feel this way as well when you are being a provider for your family. I learned the hard way through a horrific car accident (I will talk more about this is my upcoming book "From Rejected to Redeemed) the importance of self-love/self-care.

Understand that self-care isn't selfish or self-centered. It is necessary for you to live a balanced life. I had lived so much of my life looking out for everyone else, taking in the homeless, sacrificing my wants so others could have their needs met that somehow I chose myself less and less. By putting my needs on the back burner, it took a toll on my love of self.

I had to learn how to take care of me. My car accident was a wake-up call showing me how unbalanced my life had become. It became clear very quickly who my real family and friends were. I went from having a crowd at my home on a weekly basis to not knowing who I could call on for help.

When you get so accustomed to operating in a certain way, it becomes second nature for you. I had spent so much of my life working to get people to love me that I didn't realize I was still doing it until after my car accident. Depression started to creep back in. See by this time, I thought I was already comfortable in my own skin. I had went through the all the steps to becoming comfortable in my skin. But, I had to face the harsh reality that I had allowed some of the very things I had been delivered from to come back into my life.

I realized that if I wanted to remain on this path to becoming comfortable in my own skin, I had to put some measures in place to ensure that I had continued growth. I had to keep asking myself the hard questions. I had to continue to look myself in the mirror. I had to take off all the masks that I had collected over the course of my life.

It's always good to do a self-reflection assessment from time to time. By doing this, it will help you keep your priorities straight and maintain balance in your life. There is absolutely nothing wrong with being there for others, but make sure you Take time to take care of YOU first! As you develop a relationship with God, He will help you balance everything out.

Forgive yourself for not doing it in the past. Make sure that loving yourself is a priority. Get your hair done, get pampered with a manicure and pedicure, take a day to simply do nothing and relax, check off your bucket list, or get a massage. Develop better eating habits, exercise get your priorities in order, stop taking on more than you can handle, say no, and get some rest!

On the following page you will see a self-assessment that I came up with for myself to help me continue on my path to becoming comfortable in my own skin. I believe that this self-assessment will help you on your journey too. You may not completely understand the purpose of the questions initially. Prayerfully by the end of the book, everything will come together and make sense.

Self-Reflection Assessment

1. Have you accepted Jesus as your personal Lord and Savior?

2. If you answered yes, do you have a devoted time each day for Bible study and prayer? If no, why not?

3. Do you worship God with your life daily? Explain.

4. Is there anything in your life more important than your relationship with God? Explain.

5. Do you apply the Biblical principles to your daily life? Explain.

6. Do you honor God in every area of your life (work, school, and, home)? Would a

stranger know you were a Christian just by watching you?

7. Do you share your testimony with others about what God has done and is doing in your life? Why/why not?

8. Do you pray and ask God how you can be more useful in his kingdom? Explain.

9. Do you find the most pleasure, significance, and security in God? Or do you find those things in your job, spouse, or material possessions? Explain.

Please take a look at the charts on the next page then answer the last two questions:

- You always put others first. Other people's view of you is important. You can't sense God's presence.

- You put God before anyone else. You do what God requires of you because you love him. You have an intimate relationship with God.

- You attend worship service when you have time or are made to. You go to church to get a blessing.

- Christ is the center of your life. You are the church. You attend worship service to bless God. Your relationship with God is an act of worship.

- You go with your gut feelings. You have addictive behaviors to cope with your problems.

- You allow the Holy Spirit to guide you daily, resulting in harmony with God's plan.

10. Which description above best represents your life? Left or Right?

11. What are you willing to do to get your life more in harmony with God's plan?

Chapters 23-32

Fall, Get Up, Repeat
The Being Mary Jane
Years

*"For I am about to fall, and my
pain is ever with me."*
Psalm 38:17

I continued the same pattern for a
number of years: fall, get up,
repeat! Going from relationship to
relationship, not realizing that I
was allowing my pain to rule me.
Making the same mistakes over
and over again thinking that the
results would be different. Insane
right? In my mind, it seemed that
the next time my plan would be
better than the last time. But, I
had to keep repeating the test
until I learned the lessons.

After having my son at age 17, I
made it my goal in life to prove
everybody wrong about me. I was
not a failure. I was somebody! My
life wasn't over just because I had

a baby. I put sticky notes with scriptures and inspirational quotes all over my bathroom mirror. I thought to myself, I can be successful. And I don't need a man to do it! Besides, all the men in my life were a disappointment with the exception of my Grandfather.

I became an independent woman who worked full-time, secured a scholarship to pay for college; all while taking care of my son. By the time I finished college, I had landed a pretty good job. I thought to myself, you did it. You have made something of yourself. I had proven everybody wrong about me. I was somebody! Deep down, I still wasn't happy.

After being told by so many friends and family that I was being too hard on men, I decided to give love another try. We were only married for 2 weeks and my husband decided to leave me and go back to his old girlfriend. I had our marriage annulled. God had already told me 3 times not to marry him in the first place, so I felt like this was punishment for my disobedience. I thought, God is still the same harsh God He has always been. Here is goes judging and punishing me again. He has been punishing me since my birth. I asked God, why did you create me? I just don't understand! I felt so hopeless. All of my plans to get love still didn't work.

I went to the church for help, but they didn't seem to care to get involved. All they could say was you never should've married him in the first place. This was very true but, I told you so wasn't going to help me with this current dilemma. I started seeing a psychologist who prescribed me an anti-depressant. I asked to be transferred to another city, hoping to get a fresh start and get my life back on track. Once my ex-husband got word that I had moved, he pursued me.

I learned early on that you had to have your act together or at least look the part so you could be accepted by people. It didn't matter what was really going on in your life. So I decided that at all costs, I was going to make my marriage work to prove people wrong about me and to finally get that love I so desperately desired. I took him back and we remarried.

That same year we took a trip to Las Vegas. While on this trip, my husband taught me how to play blackjack. I didn't really care too much for it until we returned home. He started wanting to go to the casino near our house. I would go with him, but wouldn't gamble. Until one day, I was bothering him so much that he sent me away to play something just to leave him alone. To appease him, over the next couple months we gambled on a weekly basis. He would win, I would lose. Eventually we decided that we weren't going to gamble anymore. We wanted to get back into church.

We were both raised in a church environment, so we knew that we were heading down the wrong road. We entered counseling and decided to have a baby in hopes that it would bring us closer together. I became pregnant that summer.

Again, he decided to leave me for another woman. I was in a vicious cycle of dysfunction. My marriage had become a revolving door. He would come and go as he pleased just like God, my Father, and every other man that had come into my life. During the 2 weeks he was gone this time, I went into labor and lost our baby. I thought, surely God was punishing me for having all those abortions in my late teens and early twenties.

My husband came back again and we decided to work things out. Everything was going fine until the following year when I became pregnant with our daughter. He decided again that he didn't want to be married anymore and he left. Shortly after he left, I was hospitalized and bedridden for the whole pregnancy.

Thoughts went through my head ranging from making myself miscarry to giving her up for adoption. I even went as far and checking into adoption because I didn't want to raise another child on my own.

By this time, my Mother had become a prayer warrior. Her faith in God kept me from doing either one. The prayers of the righteous avail. My baby girl arrived early at thirty weeks. After she was in the NICU two weeks, I convinced the doctors to let me bring her home. She continued to thrive. You would never know that she was a preemie. She was one of the many miracles that God used to reveal Himself to me.

After repeated attempts to get my husband to come home, I finally got up the nerve to get an attorney to file a petition for child support. My husband hadn't visited his daughter nor would he acknowledge her. Sound familiar? During the course of the child support hearings, my husband brought evidence to court stating that we were already divorced. We had gone to see an attorney about getting custody of his other two children a year earlier. My husband in one of his disappearing acts went and asked the attorney to change the custody papers to divorce papers. In my anger, I rushed to sign the divorce papers.

In our many break ups and make ups, we called the attorney and told him that we wanted to remain married and no longer wanted to go through with the divorce. But when my husband decided to leave again, he called the attorney back and told them to go ahead and process the divorce papers. I never knew of this incidence until we were in court for child support. Can you imagine the shocker?

I was so ashamed, embarrassed, and humiliated. To save face, I told people that these hearings were part of my divorce proceedings. In actuality, he was claiming that he wasn't the father and we were already legally divorced!

Sound familiar? My plans were getting better right? At least he married me? I would soon learn the hard way. Every time you play on the devil's playground, you gone get burnt!

I always had a successful career and everyone looked to me for guidance and financial assistance. So I buried myself back into work since that was the only thing I seemed to be good at. On the surface everything seemed ok. But deep down, I had some serious mental issues still going on that I didn't want to face nor did I want anyone to know about. I started taking anti-depressants again. I was still trying to be this independent woman that had it all together. This is what everyone expected of me and the only way I could keep their love. I had to keep my life under control.

The stress of having a new baby, no husband, a considerably lower income, being a single mother again, and trying to be everything to everybody only put me in a deeper depression. I had been off work for over 6 months, so I had already started dipping into our savings and 401k. When my husband left so did his wallet. Soon I started gambling as a way to cope with the loss of my husband and the loss of income.

Gambling reminded me of the good times we had. This reminder turned into a full-blown problem. I did really well for a while, but eventually my luck ran out. Not only did I give back over $200,000 that I had won, I had maxed out all my credit cards, took out personal lines of credit, and loans to support my habit. I went from not being able to get the love I so desperately desired, to spending all of my hard earned money to get back a good feeling that would never return.

I began to sink into a deeper depression because all my coping mechanisms weren't working anymore. My career, food, nor sex could get me out of this funk. Now I had a gambling problem. I tried to seek help only to find out that nothing had changed. People could care less what's really going in your life as long as it's not complicating their life.

My family (church family included) that I thought loved and cared for me could care less about what I was going through. As long as I was winning and contributing to their life, they didn't look at it as a problem. But, when I started losing, they got busy talking about me behind my back and distancing themselves from me. No one tried to give a solution to my problem. Why should they? It wasn't their problem. I had made my own bed hard, so I had to sleep in it.

My Mother used to always ask me, why do you always have a house of full of people? My response was because I love to entertain. She would always tell me that people didn't care anything about me, they just liked what I could do for them. Little did I know at the time, she was absolutely right! I had always been there for everyone else over the years, but no one was there for me. I had tried to be a good church member, friend, sister, cousin, aunt, daughter, and mother. At the end of the day, I still wasn't loved and accepted by anyone!

I was growing very tired of my life. I wanted to get my control back. I had lost all of my money so the only way I could move forward was to gamble, kill myself, or get rid of my house. My home burned and I found myself wanting to gamble even more. I was turning into someone I didn't like. A person with evil intentions. My life had become completely unmanageable.

While I was gambling, my Mother was murdered. I was supposed to spend the weekend with her, but changed my plans at the last minute. The guilt of feeling like I should've been there sent me into a complete tailspin.

I seriously considered suicide many times, but I knew that I couldn't leave my children like that. I couldn't figure out a way to do it and make sure my children were taken care of. Then, I contemplated killing all of us. This was my lowest point. The faith I learned from my Mother kicked in and I decided to check myself into a behavioral health program to get help with my depression and gambling problems.

At this point, I hadn't even thought about my food addiction. I had went from 135 lbs to over 200 lbs. My life was a complete and utter mess. I didn't love myself, sought to find love in others, tried to control how people saw me so they would love me. Could my life get any worse?

But God! He always has a plan. I still didn't realize it at the time, but I soon would. All those years of feeling rejected began to make sense now. I was still that little baby in the beginning crying out for people to help me, wanting someone to save me from drowning in the sorrow of my pain. All that rejection was a redirection to the only ONE who could help me God!

After being in the hospital for one week, I realized that they couldn't help me. I realized no medicine, no doctor, no human, nothing could help me, but God! While lying in my hospital bed, medications hid under my pillow; I finally had reached the end of my rope!

Questions for Reflection

Did you notice I had begun to think positive?

Did you notice the effect positive thinking had on my professional life?

Did you notice that as great as positive thinking is, I still needed more?

Did you notice the vicious cycle I was in?

Have you ever been in a cycle of repeated behavior?

I used sex, food, gambling, and my career to cope with life. Do you having any coping mechanisms that you use to get through life? What did you do to break the cycle?

Do you watch the show "Being Mary Jane"?
Do you understand why I call this period in my life the "Being Mary Jane years"? Explain.

Have you ever been tired of being tired? At the end of your rope? Explain.

What was your solution?

Step 5

Embrace your "Personality Flaws"

"People will always have different views about you, just make sure you're giving them a good view."
Tuwana Nicole

Everybody can't be charismatic, easy going, laid back, or just get along with everyone. I have been told from the time that I can remember that I talk too much. I was looking back at my yearbook and some school mates wrote that I was always talking and that many times I gave my opinion without being asked. For many years it bothered me that people looked at me that way. I struggled for years thinking there was something wrong with me because I liked to talk so much.

Most people would rather hear, tell, and live a lie instead of just being real. Be willing to accept the good, the bad, and ugly about your personality. But, also be willing to make the necessary adjustments when your personality is harmful or hurtful toward others. I am thankful for my classmates being honest with me because it made me seek my Creator (God) about it.

As I began to mature and get to know who Tuwana was, I realized there was nothing wrong with me talking all the time. The difference now is that when I speak, I speak with purpose. I no longer simply run my mouth just to be talking, but I use my voice to stand for truth, love, and understanding.

This was the way God made me (a natural born leader, entrepreneur, motivational speaker, counselor, and advocate). I have always had some positive and encouraging things to say, but I had allowed my desire to be loved and accepted to hinder my ability to accept that part of my personality and I struggled to take my own advice.

We all have flaws and I encourage you to embrace yours. There are parts of our personalities that people will like and parts that they won't like. I encourage you to ask God what parts of your personality He would like for you to work on. Ask Him to show you what His purpose is for your perceived flaws. Sometimes what the next person may consider a flaw, God designed specifically for you to fulfill the purpose He has for your life.

Never let anyone tell you to dull yourself so they can shine more brightly. God made us all different and unique and there is enough room for all of us to shine with the personality God gave us. Make sure that you're always giving people something good to talk about even if they don't necessarily like your personality. Keep giving them a good view!

Questions for Reflection

Do you have some personality "flaws" that you don't like? Explain.

Are they hurtful/harmful to yourself and others?

Have you asked God why He made you the way He did?

Overall, how do you feel about yourself? Explain.

Step 6

Embrace Your "Physical Flaws"

"Beautiful girl, learn to be comfortable in your own skin."
Tuwana Nicole

Everybody can't be a supermodel, have the longest hair, or flawless skin. Accept yourself just the way God made you. God made all of us unique and special in our own way to Him. Growing up in an environment where I never felt loved and accepted, I struggled with my physical "flaws."

With today's technology advancements with plastic surgery, weave, booty lifts, breast implants, and injections; you have the ability to have whatever look you want. But, I would encourage you to make sure you're doing it for yourself and not to please anyone else. Also don't do it to make yourself more acceptable or to fit in. Definitely, don't go into to debt or beyond your financial means.

I grew up with self-esteem issues that I didn't begin to break through until after I began to develop a relationship with God. It took me years to get over my feelings of inadequacy due to the name calling I had encountered as a child. But guess what, I got over all it! From the gap in my teeth, my thickness, my nose, and my breasts; I have learned to accept myself flaws and all!

I encourage you to accept your "physical flaws". If you were born short, accept it or wear shoes with a lift or heel. If you're overweight, lose weight. If you're skinny, gain weight. If you don't like your hair, change it.

At the end of the day, you need to be able to look yourself in the mirror and love yourself unconditionally with or without any of those enhancements. Because if you're not comfortable in your own skin, it will show through any enhancement that you attempt to make on your body. Remember if you don't accept yourself, who will?

Questions for Reflection

Were you teased about your body
as a child? Adult?
How did it make you feel?

Does it affect the way you feel
about yourself now? Explain.

Do you wish you could change
some of your physical "flaws"?
Explain.

Do you want or feel the need to
change to appease someone else?
Explain.

If you couldn't make any
enhancements to your body,
would it affect your self-esteem?
Why/why not?

Part 3

The Soul

The soul is the essence or embodiment of one's total self.

"Follow me and I'll show you how. Self-help is no help at all. Self-sacrifice is the way, my way, to finding yourself, your true self. What kind of deal is it to get everything you want but to lose yourself? What could you ever trade your soul for?"
Matthew 16:25-26 MSG

Chapters 33 and Beyond
From Rejected to Redeemed

"You're blessed when you're at the end of your rope. With less of you there is more of God and his rule."
Matthew 5:3 MSG

While lying in my hospital bed, I literally threw my hands up saying, "I have tried everything I can think of. I know that I am a smart woman, but nothing I am doing is working. I have always tried to treat people right, but nothing I do seems to please them." At that moment, I found myself at the feet of Jesus. He picked me up and told me how much he loved me and that he had given his life just for me. He told me that he understood what I was going through because he too had been rejected. He told me that what I had been searching for was right here all along, HIM!

I realized that on my best day I couldn't outsmart the devil in my own strength. He knew the power that I possessed from the beginning. He used anyone and any situation in an attempt to destroy me before I could find out who I was. But God!

From the beginning; God had always pursued me, supported me, believed in me, and been patient with me while I made a mess of my life. He was there every step of the way until I had gotten tired of being tired of trying to do things my way. It wasn't until this very moment that I could see ever so clearly. Nothing or no one had ever made me feel this way in my past.

I had known of God since I was a baby. But in all those years of going to church, I never really knew Him. This wasn't the same condemning God that I thought that he was. He told me just like the woman caught in adultery as recorded in John 8:3-11 *"Has no one condemned you? No one sir, she said. Then neither do I condemn you, Jesus declared. Go now and leave your life of sin."* I walked away with a joy unspeakable and peace that surpasses all understanding. At age 33, I officially died to the old Tuwana.

I never thought that I could have the deepest desire of heart quenched by God. Psalm 37:4 says *"Delight yourself in the Lord and he will give you the desires of your heart."* It never really occurred to me that God was so concerned about me and what I needed. I always thought He was looking for me to perform. I'm glad I was wrong. I finally felt loved, needed, accepted, and appreciated. I had been redeemed!

Finally I could see the light at the end of the tunnel. In January 2009, I surrendered my will over to God and I have been walking with Jesus ever since. I am allowing Him to guide me, shape me, and mold me into the woman He would have me to be.

Now I understand why the Holy Spirit led me to books on breaking the cycle and looking for love in all the wrong places at the age of 12. God had His hand over me even back then, but I was just a victim of my circumstances. I realized everyone around me was struggling to get through their lives just like I was. There was no way for them to help me if they could barely manage their own lives.

The past couple years of my life have been some of the most painful years of my life, but I can honestly say that they have been more than worth it because now I know who I am and whose I am. As a result of my healing, I am no longer ashamed of my past. God has turned my weaknesses into strengths to witness to others about the saving power of Jesus.

God showed me that He wanted me to be an encouragement to others who were hurting, especially my family because all of us were going through the same cycle of dysfunction. I no longer looked around for someone to help me and love me like I did the first 32 years of my life. I finally realized that God has always been and always will be my provider, protector, healer, and lover of my soul.

God gave me a vision in August 2009 to start a ministry called To God Be the Glory Ministries with the theme, "Nurturing the Mind, Body, and Soul." The ministry takes the holistic approach, embracing the whole person, not just the spiritual side. Our Mission is to bring glory and honor to God by lending a helping hand to those in surrounding communities, and the world over who are in need of food, shelter, clothing, family, and most importantly Jesus.

Since 2009 we have housed over 70 families, assisted over a thousand people with getting other resources, given out Bibles, devotionals, CDs, and DVDs, witnessed over 30 people give their lives to the Lord including my daughter Kennedy, and witnessed countless Christians rededicate their lives to the Lord. Never in a million years would I have thought that God would use a broken person like me to reach so many people.

Do I have it all together? Absolutely not! I have had and still have some struggles because I'm still getting accustomed to allowing the Holy Spirit to lead me. But I am happy to tell you that I no longer look for love. I love myself unconditionally, flaws and all and I turn to God every day for everything! I am a woman

becoming comfortable in my own
skin!

"*I am forgetting what is
behind and straining toward
what is ahead, I press on
toward the goal to win the
prize for which God has
called me heavenward in
Christ Jesus.*"
Philippians 3:13-14
NIV

Questions for Reflection

Did you notice that I was just like a baby every time I would cry out for help? Can you relate? Explain.

Do you understand why my thinking was like that of a baby? Explain.

Have you ever had a personal encounter with God (Jesus)? Explain.

How did that encounter impact your life?

Do you feel like you have been
redeemed (saved)? Why/why not?

What can you take from my story
to help you get to the next level in
your life? Explain.

Step 7

Develop a Relationship With God

"You become comfortable in your own skin when you know who you are because of WHOSE you are!"
Tuwana Nicole

"But seek first His Kingdom and his righteousness and all these things will be given to you as well."
Matthew 6:33 NIV

The key ingredient to becoming comfortable in your own skin is going back to your Creator: God! God will help you find your identity, worth, value, and purpose in Him. Only through a relationship with God will you truly learn who and whose you are.

If you don't take time to do this, you will never know your worth and continue to recycle the same experiences. You will continue to attract those who will reject and mistreat you because you struggle with loving yourself.

Even though I had cried out to God all of my life, I never took the time to really listen to His voice. I struggled with discerning His voice from everyone around me and my own desires. From the time I came out my Mother's womb, I struggled with why God even created me. Not understanding the why led me to not trust God as a baby. I couldn't wrap my mind around why He would allow so many horrible things to happen to me. I allowed my limited reasoning skills to overpower all the times that God was pursuing me.

Realize that when you rebel against God you are actually enslaving yourself. The freedom you think you have is only a dead-end! If you don't know how to love yourself, take time to ask God. Otherwise, the world will continue to lead you on a path of self-destruction.

There is a common misconception that we need to have everything together to be right with God. The reality is, we will never get right without God. When we to try to live life without God, we will always experience emptiness, discontentment, and depression. Developing a relationship with God won't negate who you are, it will only enhance who you are supposed to be.

Developing a relationship with God has helped me to understand His Sovereignty. Everything He does has a purpose and a plan. He gives us freewill, but He continues to pursue us regardless of our behavior. Just like he pursued me in spite of me, He pursues those who hurt me too! He knew all the things that I went through would help shape and mold me into the woman I am today. I had to go through to get through, and to be able share with you!

When you have problems with your car, you take it to the dealership right? Well the same thing applies to us as humans. When we have a problem, why not go to the one who created us. God knows our every thought, action, desire, and feeling. He is more than able to help us with ANY problem that we are experiencing. Take time with your Creator because He is the only One who can truly show you why He created you. Trust God to take care of you. Don't limit what He can do in your life based on your limited understanding of Him.

Even though I had begun to think positive, get to know myself, take care of myself, embrace my mental and physical "flaws"; it wasn't until I truly began seeking a relationship with God that all the pieces began to fall into place. I would see some change before developing a relationship with God, but never enough to keep me going in the right direction. God was glue that made everything stick together.

As long as I used my limited understanding of who God was, I continued to be defeated by my past, what others thought of me, and all of the hurt I had experienced. Finally realizing that God knew me better than I knew myself, helped me to break free and truly become comfortable in my own skin.

My decision to develop a relationship with God helped me to change. No longer was I operating in my own strength, trying to obey man-made doctrine, looking for love and acceptance, worrying about what people thought about me. Finally I was able to hear God's voice and believe what He thought about me and what His purpose for my life was.

It doesn't matter our circumstances, how we feel, or what others think. God's greatest desire is for His children (yes, you and I) to believe in Him and His Word. Developing a relationship is much easier than one would be led to think. After being in church for many years, hearing, and trying to follow different doctrines; my relationship was only developed through prayer and active listening to God.

It had always seemed impossible to please God before. Once I had my encounter with God, I began praying, and actively listening to His direction. Everything became easier. I was able to obey Him more because I understood His love for me. I could hear His voice clearly. He showed me how to be a woman after His heart. He directed to scriptures daily and gave me understanding of scriptures I hadn't even read yet.

I am no longer looking for direction because I have a relationship with the Director! I am no longer looking for acceptance because I finally realized He had accepted me all along! I no longer worry about what people think about me because God's opinion is the only one that matters! I no longer feel inadequate because He has shown me that I can do all things when I follow His lead! I am no longer look for love because I have a relationship with the lover of my soul!

We can't receive what we don't believe! If God said it, that settles it! If God promised it, believe it, and set out to achieve it! Life may not be a fairytale, but with God's guidance, you don't have to continue living a nightmare.

By developing a relationship with God and allowing Him to be the Lord of your life, you will no longer worry about how your life is going to turn out, who's going to love you, how successful you will be, how your bills will be paid, or ANYTHING! Know that God has a plan for your life so humbly walk in it.

"Therefore I tell you, whatever you ask for in prayer, believe that you have received it, and it will be yours."
Mark 11:24 NIV

"Oh yes, you shaped me first inside, then out; you formed me in my mother's womb. I thank you, High God-you're breathtaking! Body and soul, I am marvelously made!"
Psalm 139:13-14 MSG

Questions for Reflection

Do you believe that all God wants is for you to pray, actively listen, and obey to Him? Why/why not?

Do you believe you have to follow a certain set of rules to develop a relationship with God? Explain.

If so, are you following those rules? How is that working for you?

Are taking everything to God in prayer and actively listening for His answer?

If not, what are you going to do differently?

Step 8

Forgiveness

"People can't give you what they don't have so stop putting unrealistic expectations on them."
Tuwana Nicole
For if you forgive other people when they sin against you, your heavenly Father will also forgive you."
Matthew 6:14 NIV

It has been said that forgiveness is like setting a prisoner free, realizing the prisoner was you! This is a very true statement. Even though I had developed a relationship with God, I had to learn how to forgive myself and others.

Having lived through many horrific situations, experienced so much heartache and pain at the hands of people that should've been loving me; I had become bitter. God began to show me that those who hurt me were hurting too! Hurt people, hurt people. I realized that they couldn't give me what they didn't have. Not excusing what they did, but simply understanding that they were operating the best they could at the time. I had to stop expecting them to make things right or apologize. As I began to sit in my own truth, I had to do the same for those who hurt me. I realized that I had to pray for them and become more like God and forgive them. Knowing that God had forgiven me and wasn't holding my wrongs against me, made it easier to forgive those who had hurt me.

The hardest task was learning to forgive myself. I had to realize that I was still holding myself responsible for the things that happened to me when I was a child and all the subsequent bad choices that I made as a result of my lack of self-love. I had to let go and let God. I was determined not to go back to the way my life was. It took some time, but by walking hand and hand with God daily, I have forgiven myself!

I encourage you to let go of what was and create the life that you desire. I realize that the truth hurts, but the blessing comes when you allow the truth to change you for the better! Life is too short! Stop allowing your past to dictate your future. Trust the process and let God guide you. The very things we want to change in others are the very things that we need to change in ourselves. Give people the benefit of the doubt. If you want love, give love. If you want support, be supportive. If you want a friend, be a friend. If you want forgiveness, you must forgive!

I encourage you to take stock of your life and if there is anyone that you are holding a grudge against, pray for that person and ask God to help you to forgive them so you can live better than blessed! Most importantly, forgive yourself and live life to the fullest every day. Above all love others deeply!

Remember one generation's compromise is always the next generation's standard. Be the change in the world that you would like to see! Your children are watching....

Questions for Reflection

Are you finding it difficult to forgive someone who has hurt you? Explain.

Have you prayed for them? Why/why not?

Do you want God to forgive you for the things you have done wrong in your life? Why/why not?

Have you forgiven yourself?
Why/why not?

Do you believe that your life is
having a negative impact on your
children? What are actively doing
to ensure you don't repeat the
same cycle?

Conclusion

Get Comfortable Being Uncomfortable

Get comfortable with being uncomfortable because that is where growth lives. You will never become comfortable in your own skin until you get completely uncomfortable with your life the way it is. We live in a fallen world and it is of utmost importance to remain connected to our Heavenly Father. Our culture is set up in such a way that we are doomed to fail if we follow the ways of it.

It's very difficult to become comfortable in your own skin if you allow society to shape you. From the music that you listen to; the movies and shows that you watch. They can have subtle effects on your life. If you aren't careful, you'll be justifying a lifestyle you know is contrary to the will of God. Public opinion changes with the season and is thereby unreliable, but God's Word has stood the test of time.

I get it, we all like a little excitement and entertainment in our lives, but we must have some balance. Some people are satisfied with whatever looks, but remember that God is satisfied with what is good! You should get so comfortable with being uncomfortable that you will not tolerate anything that will have a negative effect on your life or that of your offspring.

You will remember how hard it was to overcome your childhood issues, past hurts, broken relationships, and how hard you fought to become the person that you are today. So you wouldn't dare go back to being selfish, manipulative, having hidden agendas, being two-faced, petty, and angry, a hater, thinking you're better, or a gossip!

Here are a few signs that you are becoming comfortable in your own skin:

1. You will have a positive outlook on life.
2. You will know yourself because you know God.
3. You will love yourself.
4. You will take care of yourself.
5. You will find it easier to forgive others because you have been forgiven.

6. You don't feel the need to compare yourself to others.

7. You will accept responsibility for your life choices and make changes for the better.

8. You are beginning to accept how you look, how much you weigh, have a healthy self-esteem, and like where you're at in life. At your core, you should feel that you are good enough just the way God made you.

9. You won't feel the need to do things simply to impress others. You can have a crowd of people around you or be by yourself and still be good.

10. You will do what you can to help others.

11. You will Pray and walk by faith daily.

12. You will acknowledge, affirm, and appreciate how far you have come and continue to move forward daily.

I am so thankful that God never gave up on me and He will never give up on you either! I thank Him for helping me to realize that I didn't have to continue going through life feeling starved of love. Now everything is simply an overflow of the love that I have received from God. I can put my full trust and confidence in knowing that God has an everlasting love for me.

Never underestimate the power of prayer. I absolutely love the fact that I don't have to go through anyone or anything to get to God! I get to experience God's presence every day, not just on Sunday! It's amazing what positive thinking can do. By changing my thinking, all of my dreams are coming true! In spite of my overwhelming personal traumatic experiences of molestation, low self-esteem, domestic violence, divorce, the murder of my Mother, financial ruin, homelessness, depression, and being deathly ill; I have risen above it all to become a beacon of hope for others. None of the things I have accomplished today would have become possible without me finally becoming comfortable in my own skin. Guess what you can too!

No matter what you choose to do in life: become an entrepreneur, seek a romantic relationship, start a non-profit, or a ministry; your level of success will be directly tied to you being comfortable in your own skin. Seek relationships of every type that will encourage you to walk more closely with God and hold you accountable to your commitment to Him.

I hope that my stories have been a source of encouragement and have helped you to surrender your life to God so you can begin your journey to becoming comfortable in your own skin!

"Examine yourselves to see whether you are in the faith; test yourselves. Do you not realize that Christ Jesus is in you-unless, of course, you fail the test? And I trust that you will discover that we have not failed the test. Now we pray to God that you will not do anything wrong-not so that people will see that we have stood the test but so that you will do what is right even though we may seem to have failed."

2 Corinthians 13:5-7 NIV

Give Yourself a Few Months, Then take the Self-Assessment again to monitor your progress. It is on the next pages so you can compare where you are now versus where you were when you began reading the book.

Self-Reflection Assessment

1. Have you accepted Jesus as your personal Lord and Savior?

2. If you answered yes, do you have a devoted time each day for Bible study and prayer? If no, why not?

3. Do you worship God with your life daily? Explain.

4. Is there anything in your life more important than your relationship with God? Explain.

5. Do you apply the Biblical principles to your daily life? Explain.

6. Do you honor God in every area of your life (work, school, and, home)? Would a

stranger know you were a Christian just by watching you?

7. Do you share your testimony with others about what God has done and is doing in your life? Why/why not?

8. Do you pray and ask God how you can be more useful in his kingdom? Explain.

9. Do you find the most pleasure, significance, and security in God? Or do you find those things in your job, spouse, or material possessions? Explain.

Please take a look at the charts on the next page then answer the last two questions:

- You always put others first. Other people's view of you is important. You can't sense God's presence.

- You put God before anyone else. You do what God requires of you because you love him. You have an intimate relationship with God.

- You attend worship service when you have time or are made to. You go to church to get a blessing.

- Christ is the center of your life. You are the church. You attend worship service to bless God. Your relationship with God is an act of worship.

- You go with your gut feelings. You have addictive behaviors to cope with your problems.

- You allow the Holy Spirit to guide you daily, resulting in harmony with God's plan.

10. Which description above best represents your life? Left or Right?

11. What are you willing to do to get your life more in harmony with God's plan?

Positive Life Quotes

"Happiness doesn't depend upon who you are or what you have, it depends solely on what you think."-Dale Carnegie

"God doesn't knit pick me, He hand-picked me."-Tuwana Nicole

"Become that which you seek."-Osho

"When we feed our faith, our doubts will starve to death."-Tuwana Nicole

"Love recognizes no barriers, it jumps hurdles, leaps fences & penetrates walls to arrive at it's destination full of hope."-Maya Angelou

You can't have faith without works you must have a faith that works!"-Tuwana Nicole

"We celebrate the past to awaken the future."-JFK

"It's not the load that breaks you down. It is the way you carry it."-Lou Holtz

"In a world full of imposters, be yourself!"-Tuwana Nicole

Positive Life Quotes

"Rejection puts you out of your comfort zone which is usually when you're at your best." – Stewart Stafford

"When we learn how to give without hesitation, forgive like there is no tomorrow; then we truly know the meaning of love."-Tuwana Nicole

"Act as if what you do makes a difference. It does."-William James

"Everyone is blessed, but those who do the will of God are better than blessed."-Tuwana Nicole

"There is no passion to be found playing small-in settling for a life that is less than the one you are capable of living."-Nelson Mandela

"A wise man learns from his mistakes, but an even wiser man learns from others mistakes."-Tuwana Nicole

"If you just set out to be liked, you would be prepared to compromise on anything at any time, and you would achieve nothing."-Margaret Thatcher

Positive Life Quotes

"Don't just survive, thrive."-Tuwana Nicole

"Man was made for God and he will never find happiness until he finds it in the ONE who made him."-Augustine

"People can't give you what they don't have."-Tuwana Nicole

"Falsehood has an infinity of combinations, but truth has only one mode of being.-Jean Jacques Rousseau

"Make today's decisions with eternity in mind."-Tuwana Nicole

"Life has no limitations, except the ones you make."-Les Brown

"Choice, not chance, determines your destiny."-Aristotle

"Being better than blessed is having joy in spite of your circumstances while embodying the courage and strength to do and be the impossible because of your relationship with God."-Tuwana Nicole

Notes

Notes

Contact
Better Than Blessed
Enterprises:

If this book has helped you in any way, we would like to hear from you. Please write or fill out a contact us form with your personal testimony. If you need prayers and/or counseling, feel free to contact us.

P.O. Box 38165
Germantown, TN 38183

OR

821 Herndon Ave Suite 141433
Orlando, FL 32814

www.betterthanblessed.com
800-736-0854
901-550-9530 Emergency Line

About the Author

Tuwana Nicole earned a bachelor's degree in Business Management from Lambuth University now University of Memphis and a certification in Biblical Counseling from Light University. She is a member of the American Association of Christian Counselors. She is also a certified travel consultant and certified hydration specialist.

Tuwana is passionate about helping others come to know God and has committed her life to serving God. She spends her time investing in the lives of others by counseling and mentoring, teaching, singing, and sharing her story.

Tuwana is the Visionary of Better Than Blessed Enterprises. BTBE services include counseling, vacation planning, health & wellness, business consultation, motivational speaking, and apparel.

Tuwana hopes that her story will inform, inspire, and encourage all people everywhere to surrender their lives to God so they can live better than blessed!

Other Available Books

Living Better Than Blessed:

A Daily Devotional to Nurture the Mind, Body, and Soul & The Living Better Than Blessed Prayer Journal

100 day devotional that you will be able help your daily walk with God.

From Rejected to Redeemed

This book will give a more in depth look at Tuwana's life and she overcame the plan of the Enemy.

Order each book at a Discounted Rate at:

betterthanblessed.com
tuwananicole.com

Better Than Blessed Enterprises Logo Meaning

The three circles represent the Mind, Body, and Soul of every individual.

Each of the colors represent the different sides to every individual:

Turquoise represents friendship, open communication, emotional balance, stability, peace, and tranquility.

Pink represents unconditional love of one self, nurture, playfulness, compassion, thoughtfulness, sensitivity, and caring.

Purple represents royalty, imagination, spirituality, and the union of the Mind, Body, and Soul.

Our sincere prayer is that our products and services will help you recognize and tap into each side of your being and live a better than blessed life.

www.betterthanblessed.com

Made in the USA
Middletown, DE
19 November 2021